W9-BMF-300

WORLD BOOK
looks at

THE AGE OF
KNIGHTS AND CASTLES

World Book, Inc.
a Scott Fetzer Company
Chicago London Sydney Toronto

WORLD BOOK
looks at
THE AGE OF KNIGHTS AND CASTLES

World Book looks at
Books in this series are based on information and illustrations contained
in The World Book Encyclopedia.

Created and edited by Brian Williams and Brenda Williams.
Designed by Tim Mayer.

World Book, Inc.
525 W. Monroe
Chicago, Illinois 60661

For information on other World Book
products, call 1-800-255-1750 x3771.

ISBN 0-7166-1801-X (hard cover)
ISBN 0-7166-1807-9 (soft cover)
Library of Congress Catalog Card Number 96-62476

Printed in Mexico

1 2 3 4 5 6 7 8 9 10 99 98 97 96

CONTENTS

Introducing the Age of Knights and Castles

Long ago, before there were cars, planes, computers, or television sets, knights rode out from castles to do battle. This happened in the period that historians call the Middle Ages – the centuries between ancient and modern times in western Europe.

People work in the fields near a castle that looks like a fairytale palace. This painting, called *September,* is from an illuminated (decorated) book made in the 1400's for a French lord named the Duc de Berry. Work on farms varied with the seasons, as it does today.

Puzzled by a new word?

To learn the meaning of a difficult or new word, turn to the glossary on page 62.

What life was like then

In those days, most people lived in small villages, and rarely moved far from the place they were born. People in Europe knew little about Asia or Africa and nothing at all about America.

The great age of castle building in Europe lasted from about A.D. 1000 to 1500. Usually a castle belonged to a king, or to a landowner called a lord. The castle was built to keep out enemies, so it was a fortress as well as a home. Within its walls lived the lord and his best soldiers. These men wore armor and rode into battle on horseback. They were called knights.

In this book

In this book, you are taking a trip back in time. You will discover what castles were like and how people lived in the days when castles were built. You will learn how knights trained, what a knight's armor was like, and how different life was then. And you will see pictures of castles that still stand today, as reminders of those long-ago times.

The end of an age

By 1500 the age of knights and castles was over. Cannon and gunpowder could blast holes in the walls of the strongest castle. Armor was no protection against guns either, so knights no longer rode into battle wearing heavy metal suits. Columbus had sailed from Europe to America, and a new age was beginning – the Age of Exploration.

People went on building castles, but now they were used as palaces and homes for wealthy people. Today, some castles are museums, full of treasures of the past. Tourists wander through rooms where knights once ate and slept. It's fun to imagine what it was like to live in a castle or be a knight. Let's begin.

IMPORTANT EVENTS OF THE AGE OF CASTLES

476   Fall of the Roman Empire, which governed much of Europe.

570?   Birth of the prophet Muhammad, founder of Islam.

400's- Angles, Saxons, and other peoples
600   from Europe settled in England.

732   Charles Martel, leader of the Franks, defeated Muslim invaders and halted the Muslim advance into Europe.

800   Charlemagne, king of the Franks, was crowned emperor of the Holy Roman Empire, a new empire in western Europe.

800   Maya civilization in Central America reached its peak.

800's   Vikings from Scandinavia attacked England, Ireland, and other parts of western Europe.

1002   Viking explorer Leif Ericson sailed from Greenland to North America.

1066   William the Conqueror led the Normans to invade England.

1096   First Christian Crusade to the Holy Land (Palestine). The last important Crusade ended in 1270.

1206   Genghis Khan became ruler of Mongolia. After conquering much of Asia, the Mongols attacked eastern Europe in 1241.

1215   Magna Carta or the Great Charter was signed in England.

1271   Marco Polo left Italy to travel to China, and did not return until 1295.

1337- England and France fought the
1453   Hundred Years' War.

1347- A terrible disease known as the
1352   plague or Black Death swept across Europe.

1368- The Ming dynasty ruled China, after
1644   the end of Mongol rule.

1400's The Aztecs built their empire in Mexico.

1455- Civil wars known as the Wars of the
1485   Roses were fought in England.

1492   Columbus sailed to the New World. The period known as the Renaissance or "rebirth of learning" began, bringing new ideas in art and science, and an end to the Middle Ages.

Why is a castle called a castle?

The word castle comes from the Latin word *castellum.* Latin was the language spoken by the ancient Romans and a *castellum* was a Roman fort.

Who built the first castles?

Huge stone fortresses were built in Greece and Turkey more than 3,000 years ago. Walled towns developed in the Middle East about 10,000 years ago.

Who were first called knights?

The word knight comes from the Old English word *cniht,* which means a household retainer. English people used the word to describe French mounted soldiers who first came to England after the Norman conquest of 1066. These knights were warriors equipped and trained to fight on horseback.

Castles and Forts

Most of the castles still standing today were made of stone. Many such castles were built in Europe between 1000 and 1500. But long before then, people had built castles of earth and wood.

Hilltop forts and towers

People in Europe built forts on hilltops during the Stone Age, more than 5,000 years ago. These forts had walls made of turf or chalk dug out of the hillside, and they were encircled by earth banks and ditches for added protection. If an enemy attacked, the people took shelter inside the fort with their farm animals.

Later, people in Britain built brochs – stone towers with no windows and only one door. Nobody actually lived in such towers, but people may have used them as places of refuge from attacks by raiders seeking slaves.

Fort-villages

After about 450 B.C., Europeans built wooden stockade forts. The gateways of these forts were

A round tower in County Galway, Ireland. These towers look like the older stone buildings called brochs. This tower was built in the 1100's.

DID YOU KNOW?

When the Normans crossed the sea from France to invade England they brought a prefabricated wooden castle with them. It was made in sections that were quickly fitted together to make a stronghold after the landing.

The Tower of London was built by the Normans after they invaded England in 1066. William the Conqueror needed the fortress to protect and control the capital city of London. The oldest part of the famous national monument is the keep – the great central tower known as the White Tower. Later parts of the fortress were built around the White Tower.

The Bayeux Tapestry tells the story of the Battle of Hastings, where the Normans defeated the English in 1066. The tapestry is a long piece of embroidery on linen cloth. The scene below shows Norman knights on horseback charging the English, who are fighting on foot. The Bayeux Tapestry is more than 900 years old and is kept in a museum in France.

protected by banks and ditches that served as barriers, making it hard for the enemy to storm the gate. The fort's defenders stood on top of the stockade, hurling spears and stones at the enemy. People felt safe inside the hill forts and built homes within their walls. In time, the forts became walled villages.

The Romans

The Romans made many forts in Europe. They built walls around towns and erected impressive frontier defenses, like Hadrian's Wall in northern England.

The Normans

The Normans built stone castles as strongholds from which they could rule the lands they had won in battle. After they conquered England in 1066, one of the first castles they built was the Tower of London. In the 1100's the Normans invaded Ireland, and built stone castles there too.

Dover Castle in England. The keep of this famous castle was erected in the 1180's. Dover Castle stands on a cliff near the port town of Dover, facing France across the English Channel. The castle was built to defend the port against invaders.

A castle was a home, but not a very comfortable place to live. Castles were designed to make it very difficult for anyone to capture them.

The strongest part of the first Norman castles was the keep. However, some keeps were square, and if the enemy dug under one corner, the whole tower fell down. For this reason, later castles had round or many-sided keeps.

Walls and towers

Most castles had an outer wall built around the top of a hill. Inside the wall was a central courtyard, called a bailey. Towers, connected by a walkway, were added at intervals along the wall. The towers had few entrances at ground level, so each one was a strong point for defense. If the wall was damaged in an attack, or if one tower was captured, soldiers in the other towers could fight on.

Gate and moat

The keep stood in the middle of the earliest castles, at some distance from the fiercest fighting. The first attack usually came at the main entrance to the castle, so a strong gatehouse was needed. Castles built later had the keep brought forward to serve as the gatehouse. The castle commander lived in the gatehouse and directed his soldiers in battle.

A ditch dug around the outer walls provided extra protection. Often this ditch was flooded with water to make a moat. A narrow bridge called a drawbridge was the only way across the moat. The drawbridge could be raised when an enemy was sighted, so it kept invaders away from the castle walls.

Building castles

Builders chose the site of a new castle with care. They often used the same site on which earlier people had made a wooden fort. On flat land, the builders dug a ditch and piled up the soil to make a hill. Then they built their castle on top of the hill.

Where castles were built

- A good place to build a castle was on a hilltop. The castle guards could see enemy soldiers coming as they climbed the hill to attack the castle.

- Some castles were built inside cities, as palaces and fortresses.

- Many castles were built to guard rivers and roads.

A castle by the sea. This is an artist's idea of a typical castle. It has a moat filled with water (right), crossed by a drawbridge. In this castle, the strongest point is the gatehouse, with its four towers. Other large towers defend the corners of the inner wall. There is a Great Hall, a kitchen, and a chapel, as well as living quarters for knights, foot soldiers, and servants.

The Knight's Castle

A castle belonged to a nobleman or lord who probably owned the land around the castle too. The knights who fought for him also lived in the castle. They had to be ready to ride out on their horses and do battle at the lord's command.

Also living in the castle were servants who cooked the lord's food, and took care of his family. From the safety of his castle, a lord could defy his enemies – and control his own people. The same strong, stone walls that could keep out an army could keep in a prisoner, so the castle was also a jail. A castle provided a fortress base from which the lord and his knights governed the surrounding region.

A knight armed for battle. In one hand he grasps a sword and in the other he holds a shield. His body is covered by metal armor, and his head is completely covered by a helmet, so his face is hidden. Other knights knew him by the lion symbol pictured on his shield and on his horse's coverlet. The lion identified him as Guy de Dampierre, the Count of Flanders.

Alcazars

Spain has about 1,400 castles and palaces built in the Middle Ages. Many of the finest castles, built by the Moors, were beautifully decorated palace-fortresses called alcazars. Alcazar is an Arabic word meaning "fortified palace." The most famous alcazar is the magnificent Alhambra in Granada, Spain.

A Lord of Legend

The Cid, or El Cid, is a great Spanish hero. He was born about 1043 and his real name was Rodrigo Diaz de Vivar. The name El Cid means "the lord." It was given to him by Muslims from North Africa who had conquered part of Spain. These people, known as the Moors, admired El Cid, even though he fought against them.

El Cid was a knight who fought for King Sancho II of Castile, one of the Christian kingdoms of Spain. When Sancho was murdered by his hated brother Alfonso, El Cid was banished. He gathered a small army and fought for anyone who hired him.

El Cid became rich and powerful. In 1094 he took the kingdom of Valencia from the Moors. After he died in 1099, the story of El Cid became a legend told in poems and songs.

The Alhambra, a famous alcazar in Granada, is known for the beauty of its inner courtyards, such as the Court of the Lions.

A castle in Spain. This castle near Toledo was built in the 1400's. Like many castles, it stands on high ground.

Life in the castle

- The lord and his family lived in the castle.
- The lord entertained guests in the Great Hall.
- Religious services and prayers were held in the chapel.
- The lord slept on a bed. The servants slept on the floor with the dogs.
- Stone floors were usually covered with straw.
- The castle was gloomy. At night, people lit candles made of animal fat, and torches made of wood.
- In winter, people kept warm around wood fires.
- Windows had no glass. Only wooden shutters kept out the wind.
- Toilets emptied into the moat.

How People Lived

Springtime tasks on a manor are shown in this picture, called *March*, from a book of the seasons made in the early 1400's. Peasants work in the fields around the castle. The plowman is driving two oxen. Horses replaced oxen on many farms during the later Middle Ages because a horse can pull a plow three or four times faster than an ox can.

By the 800's most land in western Europe was split up into large estates ruled by rich lords. These estates were called manors. People on these lands lived in small villages – there were few towns or cities.

Most people were peasants who lived by farming. They grew crops and raised animals to feed and clothe themselves. They also worked for the lord of the manor, on whom they depended.

Lord of the manor

The lord of the manor was usually a nobleman and a knight. His job was soldiering and he took orders from his king. By pledging loyalty and promising to serve the king, the lord became the king's vassal (follower). In return, the king granted him land. This granting of land in return for service was called feudalism.

The lord controlled the land and collected taxes. He also judged disputes, kept an army of knights, and supervised the farming of his land. The feudal system lasted until the 1200's in western Europe.

Fiefs and vassals

Feudalism was a system that benefited knights and noblemen. For example, let's suppose that a nobleman, Sir John, pledged, or promised, loyalty to William the Conqueror, king of England. By doing so, Sir John became the king's vassal. He promised to supply the king with 10 knights. In return, King William gave Sir John 20 manors to rule as his fief. This meant that the land still belonged to the king, but was entrusted to the lord – Sir John.

A lord's life

- The lord lived in a manor house or a castle.

- He had a garden, an orchard, farms and farm buildings, and peasants.

- Many manors also had a church, a mill (for grinding flour), and a press for making wine from grapes and other fruits.

If the king called his army to battle, Sir John had to go, and take nine other knights with him. Sir John might have to hire "freelance" knights to make up the number. As payment, he gave each knight a manor as a fief. The knight pledged his loyalty and service to Sir John. The knight was now Sir John's vassal.

Harnessing the horse. A farmer drives horses to prepare a field for sowing seeds. The animals wear the horse-collar harness, used in Europe from the 900's. Here, they are pulling a harrow to break up lumps of soil after plowing. Nearby, an archer practices with his longbow.

A peasant's life

- Peasants lived in huts clustered near the castle.

- A peasant farmed the lord's land as well as any small plots of his own.

- He depended on the lord for protection from enemies.

- He depended on the lord to give him justice.

- Under the law, a peasant was part of a lord's property.

- If a new lord took charge of the manor, the peasants remained with the land. They were "bound to the soil."

Life on a manor. The peasants raised livestock, such as the sheep and cattle shown here, and grew crops. In this painting, a woman is milking a cow, while another woman churns butter at the door of her house.

A peasant family worked together to farm the lord's land as well as their own.

Peasants also cut wood in the forest for the lord, stored his grain at harvest time, and repaired roads and bridges. They had their own grain milled into flour at the lord's mill, baked their bread in the lord's oven, and took their grapes to the lord's wine press. Each time, they had to pay the lord. Peasants usually paid in wheat, oats, eggs, or chickens.

Home life was simple

Peasants lived in bare huts. They slept on bags filled with straw, and ate black bread, eggs, and poultry. For vegetables, they grew beans, cabbages, and turnips. Meat was a special treat. Peasants were not allowed to hunt or fish, because the wild animals, like everything else on the manor, belonged to the lord.

Changing the crops

Fields on the manor were large, and divided into strips. Each peasant worked several strips: plowing, sowing seed, and harvesting. Each family farmed strips in different parts of the fields, so that good land and bad land were shared equally.

A new cow

Farmers began to improve their plants and livestock.

- **They bred a dairy cow that gave especially rich milk.**

- **This cow, called the Guernsey, was produced in northwestern Europe about 1100 and became a prized animal. Its creamy milk makes good butter.**

Farmers grew different crops in turn in each field from one year to the next. This kept the soil fertile and helped prevent disease in plants. Farmers during the Middle Ages began to split farmland into three fields, not two as formerly. They let one field lie fallow for a season by not planting any crops in it. In the other two fields, they grew two different crops – perhaps wheat and beans. In this way, two-thirds of the land could be farmed each year, instead of only half.

Hard times

- When a peasant died, his son had to give the lord his father's best cow or sheep. Then he had to give the second-best farm animal to the local priest.

- If a peasant's daughter married someone from another village and moved away, the peasant had to pay a fine to the lord.

A village in Scandinavia during the Middle Ages. People built their houses of stone or wood. Many houses had just one room, while others were long buildings with three or more rooms. Many small farm communities grew up near rivers, where people could use boats for travel and trade.

Becoming a Knight

A knight's training began when he was a boy. Instead of going to school, he learned how to behave correctly – and how to fight.

A man could become a knight when he was about 21 years old, in either of two ways. The simplest way was on the battlefield, as a reward for bravery. Being tapped on the shoulder with a sword by another knight or a king made a man a knight.

In peacetime, a future knight had to undergo years of training. When his training was completed, he took part in a religious ceremony during which he swore to live a godly life.

From page to knight

A boy training for knighthood left home when he was about 7 years old. First, he became a page, or student, in the household of a knight or a nobleman. There he learned to handle small weapons. He also learned the code of courtesy (polite behavior) expected of a knight.

At the age of 15 or 16, a page became a squire. He acted as a servant to his lord, and rode with him into battle.

After about five years, a squire became a knight. For the religious ceremony, he took a bath, had his hair cut short, and prayed all night in church. In the morning, he received the sword and spurs of a knight.

At tournaments, knights practiced their fighting skills. In this form of mock battle, each knight aimed his long lance at the other.

The Age of Chivalry

The age of knights is often called the Age of Chivalry. Chivalry comes from the Old French word *chevalerie*, which means "horse soldiering." Over time, the term came to mean the code of behavior, or set of rules, by which a knight was expected to live. A knight who was guilty of cowardice or other serious misconduct was disgraced. His sword and his spurs were taken from him, and broken.

A knight in plate metal armor.

In real life, however, a knight did not always live up to these high ideals. Sometimes his code of honor was applied only to members of his own high rank. Knights often acted brutally toward people of lower rank or those whose lands they conquered and plundered.

The Garter story

An order of knighthood was founded by King Edward III of England around 1348. No one knows for sure how it originated but, according to legend, it began at a court ball.

The king was dancing with a noblewoman when the lady lost her garter. The king picked it up. As he did so, he saw several people smile and make remarks. He was angry, and exclaimed, *"Honi soit qui mal y pense,"* a French phrase that means "Dishonored be he who thinks evil of it." The king declared that he would make the garter "so glorious that everyone would wish to wear it." He did this by founding a new order of knighthood – the Order of the Garter – which is still the highest order of knighthood in Great Britain.

A true knight was expected to

- **protect women and the weak,**
- **champion right against injustice and evil,**
- **love the land of his birth, and**
- **defend the church, even with his life.**

A man was knighted by being tapped on the shoulder with a sword by another knight or his king.

A page learned to fight with swords. He also learned games of skill, such as chess, and hunted with trained hawks.

A squire waited on his lord at table. He tested his skill with a lance against a dummy target. In battle he rode at his master's side.

Knights in Armor

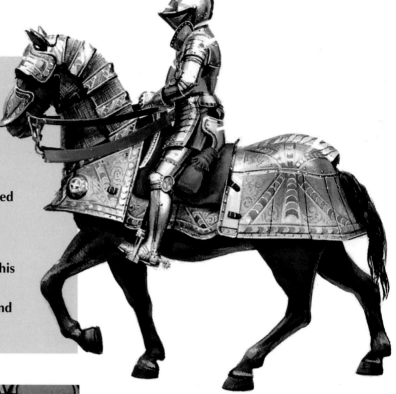

A knight in full armor

Each piece of armor was made to fit the knight's body, and each had a special name.

- On his head, the knight wore a helmet.
- The helmet had a visor that lifted up and down like a shutter.
- A collar made of chain mail protected the gap between the knight's helmet and the top of his body armor.
- The knight wore metal shoes and gloves called gauntlets.

Knights wearing surcoats over chain-mail armor. The surcoat was a tunic worn in the 1200's. This picture is from an illuminated Old Testament manuscript. Although it tells a Bible story, it shows people in the style of clothing worn when the picture was made.

When riding into battle, a knight wore a heavy suit of metal armor. Sometimes his horse was also armored. Many knights riding together made a colorful and impressive sight.

Chain mail

A knight wore armor to protect his body from arrows, swords, spears, clubs, and other weapons. The first knights wore a long garment like a dress, made of padded cloth or leather. Over that, they put on a suit of chain-mail, made from tiny metal rings linked together. A Norman knight wore a chain mail suit and a cone-shaped metal helmet. He carried a long spear, called a lance, and a shield that was large enough to protect most of his body.

Steel suits

Later, in the 1300's, helmets were stronger and covered the entire head. Knights also began wearing extra pieces of metal plate to cover vital areas that chain mail did not protect well – such as the elbow, arm, knee, and leg. By the 1400's, knights were wearing complete suits of plate armor. The suits had joints that allowed knights to walk and bend, but they were still clumsy.

Learning to wear armor

It must have been extremely hot and uncomfortable inside a suit of armor. A knight in training practiced putting on the armor (in the correct order, or the pieces would not fit), and fighting in it. He learned to leap onto the saddle of his horse wearing armor, and to ride his horse while holding a lance and shield. And he learned to fight with a knight's weapons, such as a long sword and a spiked club.

A knight wearing a metal helmet. The helmet shown here has a pointed front that deflects (turns aside) a blow. It has small holes for the knight's eyes and mouth, as well as airholes. Even so, with the visor down, it must have been stuffy inside that helmet.

A coat of mail was much too uncomfortable to wear all the time. The knight rolled it up and carried it on his horse.

A man had to be strong to wear armor. A suit of chain mail weighed about 50 pounds (23 kilograms). Plate armor was even heavier.

A Norman knight rode on a horse, but the horse had no armor. The ordinary foot soldier had only a helmet, and perhaps a shield like this round buckler.

A knight's gauntlet, or metal glove, worn around 1550.

Knights into Battle

Single combat sometimes helped decide a battle. Robert Bruce inspired his Scots followers when he beat the English knight Sir Henry de Bohun before the Battle of Bannockburn. Here, Bruce is aiming an ax blow against the English knight, who has missed the Scot with his lance thrust.

When a knight rode into battle, he hoped his armor and weapons would give him victory. Christian knights prayed that God would be on their side. Sometimes two knights faced each other in single combat, but most battles were fought between armies of knights and foot soldiers.

The battle-ax was a weapon used by knights in close combat.

Choosing the ground

The battleground was often important in deciding which side won. The Battle of Bannockburn in 1314 was one of the most important battles fought in Scotland. The Scots, led by Robert Bruce, fought from a better position. The English knights were too crowded together to use their greater numbers, and the Scots won.

Down and out

Knights charging into battle on horseback were the armored tanks of their time. They usually smashed through the enemy foot soldiers. But if a knight fell from his horse, he was out of the fight – and in trouble. His armor was so heavy that he could not get to his feet without help. If he was lucky, he was captured. If not, he was killed by the enemy. Soldiers stripped dead knights of armor and weapons and took these as trophies.

The Battle of Bannockburn. This picture was made in the 1400's, more than 100 years after the battle. It shows knights and foot soldiers fighting fiercely.

Held to ransom

A king or an important lord captured in battle seldom was killed. He was worth more alive.

- He was held prisoner until his friends paid a sum of money called a ransom.

- In exchange for the ransom, the captive was freed.

- Some prisoners had to wait many years before the ransom money was paid.

- King Richard I of England, also known as Richard the Lion-Hearted, was captured on his way home from the Crusades and held for ransom by the Duke of Austria.

Battles were often very confused. Knights were crowded together, fighting, falling to the ground, and being trampled under horses' hooves. This drawing shows the Battle of the Lech River, fought in 955, in which Otto the Great drove Hungarian invaders out of Germany.

Knights and Foot Soldiers

France and England were often at war. The French Royal Banner (above), with three fleurs-de-lis, was flown from the 1300's to the 1600's. England's King Richard I adopted the three lions (left) in 1195.

Knights against archers

The army with the largest number of knights did not always win the battle. Some famous battles between knights and foot soldiers took place during the Hundred Years' War between France and England.

The first big battle of the war was the Battle of Crécy, fought in France in 1346. English soldiers led by King Edward III defeated a much larger French army that included more than 1,000 knights. Many knights were killed by arrows.

Longbows and crossbows are seen in this picture, made in the 1300's. It shows English soldiers (right) fighting the French (left) at the Battle of Crécy in 1346. The victorious English are firing arrows from longbows. The French are preparing their crossbows to shoot back. In the actual battle, these bowmen would not have been so near each other.

At the Battle of Agincourt in 1415, about 6,000 English soldiers with longbows defeated a French army of about 30,000. In this battle, the French knights became jammed together on muddy ground and had no room to swing their swords. Thousands of French knights were struck down by arrows, while others were trampled underfoot. English losses numbered in the hundreds, but there were 10,000 dead on the French side.

Longbows against crossbows

The English and Welsh were expert bowmen or archers. Each archer carried a longbow as tall as himself.

- The bow was made of tough, springy wood, such as yew.

- The archer needed strong arms to bend his bow when he pulled back the bowstring.

- When he let the string go, the bow shot a wooden arrow at great speed.

- Longbows fired farther and faster than crossbows.

- A crossbow could fire an arrow through a thick wooden door, but the crossbowman had to wind up his weapon with a handle each time he fired.

The crossbow was a powerful weapon. These Turkish soldiers are using crank handles to draw back the strings of their crossbows for shooting.

Soldiers using pikes. Pikes were spears with long wooden handles, and a favorite weapon of Swiss foot soldiers. This picture shows the Swiss fighting the Austrians at the Battle of Sempach in 1386. The Swiss won the battle. The Austrian knights dismounted from their horses and fought on foot, which was probably why they lost.

The Knight and His Arms

A unicorn. Most coats of arms include an object or figure, like this unicorn. The unicorn was a legendary animal, with the head and body of a horse, the legs of a deer, and the tail of a lion. It had a single horn in the middle of its forehead.

Every knight had his own coat of arms – an emblem made up of pictures, colors, and symbols. Coats of arms were first displayed on the knight's shield. Later, they were shown on flags, clothes, and other personal possessions.

His coat of arms was a knight's "badge." It enabled his friends and followers to recognize him on the battlefield. Only knights had coats of arms, and they were passed on to a son and heir. No two people could have the same coat of arms.

The picture shows a knight saying farewell to his family before riding off to battle. His personal family symbols – his coat of arms – decorate his armor, horse covering, and shield.

Who's who?

When knights were covered in armor from head to foot, it took an expert to identify them by their coats of arms. The people who knew about coats of arms were called heralds. Heralds were first used to carry messages between kings or armies, and they had to know whether a knight was a friend or an enemy.

Heralds were later given the job of ruling which new design could be allowed for a coat of arms. They made sure that no two people had the same coat of arms and that no one falsely claimed to be a member of a noble family.

Buried under brass

When a knight died, his grave was often covered by a decorative brass plate. About 10,000 of these "brasses" are left in England. The oldest surviving example was made in memory of Sir John d'Aubernoun, a knight who died in 1277. It can be seen in Stoke D'Abernon, Surrey.

Most brasses date from between 1350 and 1650. They show knights in armor, sometimes pictured with their wives, and tell us much about the clothing of the time. Brasses are often set into the floors of old churches and many cover graves.

An English knight receives his helmet and shield from his wife and daughter. This illustration is based on a picture made about 1340.

Making a brass rubbing

Rubbing over the brass with wax on paper produces a copy of the picture called a brass rubbing. Many people enjoy brass rubbing as a hobby.

Swords   **Ship**   **Lion**

Charges are symbols of objects or figures on a shield. Animals were among the most popular charges.

Bendy   **Chevron**   **Lozenge**

Shields were decorated with various colors, designs, and lines that became standard – like the three shown here. Each style had a name.

A brass rubbing from a knight's tomb. Brasses that cover graves are metal plates, generally engraved with a picture of the person they commemorate.

LEGEND OF THE UNICORN

The unicorn is often shown in old paintings. It was once believed that the unicorn's horn protected people against poison. Powders said to be made of unicorn horn were sold for very high prices. Most scholars believe that the image of the unicorn was based on muddled reports of the rhinoceros.

Knights, King, and Crown

William I was crowned king of England on Christmas Day, 1066. William had won the crown by conquest when his Norman army killed the English king, Harold.

Knights served the king, who was then the supreme ruler. A noble lord might have many manors and many knights, but he was still the king's servant. Most people in those days believed that a king was God's chosen ruler on earth, so it was wrong for anyone to disobey a king.

Crowning a king

A king or a queen wore a crown as a symbol of supreme authority. Knights were present at the coronation (crowning ceremony). In Christian kingdoms, coronations took place in a church or cathedral, and included a religious service.

From the time of William the Conqueror, English kings and queens have been crowned in Westminster Abbey in London. During the ceremony, the new monarch sits in the Coronation Chair. Beneath the chair is the Stone of Scone. On this stone, Scottish kings sat to be crowned until the English king Edward I took the stone to England in 1296.

The king's champion

After a new king was crowned, he and his guests sat down to a splendid feast. A fully armed knight then rode into the banquet hall. He was the King's Champion, and challenged to a fight any person who questioned the right of the new king to rule.

Crowned heads

Crowns were worn by rulers in ancient Egypt and Assyria. The Greeks gave a crown of laurel leaves to their athletes as a symbol of victory. Roman emperors adopted this idea, but their crowns were made of metal, usually gold. Rulers in Europe probably followed the Roman custom.

Westminster Abbey in London dates from the 1000's. Kings and queens have been crowned here ever since.

Paying homage

Every knight had to pay homage to the king in order to become the king's vassal. The knight knelt before the king and placed his hands between the king's, declaring that he was the king's follower. The king then raised the knight to his feet and kissed him. The knight often swore an oath upon the Bible or upon some holy object to show that he meant to keep his promise.

Kings paid homage to other kings. Here, Edward I of England is swearing loyalty to Philip IV of France. The English king is kneeling, and places his hand on an open Bible to swear his oath.

The Coronation Chair used in the coronation of all British kings or queens is 700 years old. The wooden chair was built to hold the Stone of Scone, which can be seen beneath the seat.

The crown was a symbol of a king's power. This stained glass window of about 1200 is in Strasbourg Cathedral, France. It shows Charlemagne, a famous ruler of the Middle Ages, wearing a crown.

The King and the Law

King Henry I of England dreaming.
This picture dates from about 1140. It shows Henry asleep and having nightmares about the problems of being a king. Three angry lords threaten him with swords. Churchmen and peasants give him a list of complaints and requests.

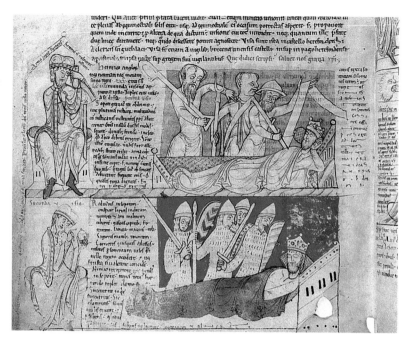

The king's judges in a court of law, known as the King's Bench. Prisoners in chains (bottom) wait to come before the judges (top). Around the table, clerks with long rolls of documents write reports of the proceedings. This picture was made about 1450.

The king and government

The king was the head of government, and his word was generally law. There was no democracy as we know it today, although the king listened to the advice of lords and churchmen meeting in council. Even so, the king was not all-powerful. He was considered bound by his people's common laws, and from these roots grew the idea of a responsible monarchy.

Law and justice

In ancient times, customs and laws often varied from district to district. In England, for example, where the laws were based on the customs of the people, similar cases were often judged differently in different districts.

In the early 1100's strong English kings began to set up a countrywide system of king's courts. Judges moved around the country to hear cases and they applied the same rulings in all similar cases. The courts set up rules known as common law that were applied equally everywhere in the country.

Crime and punishment

Laws were strict in those days. Anyone found guilty of a serious crime, such as murder, forgery, robbery, or treason could be sentenced to death. Punishment for stealing a

neighbor's chicken might be payment of a fine, branding (marking with a red-hot iron), whipping, or death. And anyone found killing deer in the king's hunting park faced almost certain death.

Dishonest shopkeepers who broke trading rules – perhaps by adding water to beer or selling underweight loaves of bread – were dragged through the streets and locked up in the town stocks. Townsfolk came to jeer and throw rotten vegetables at them.

Feudal courts settled differences among nobles. This picture shows England's King Richard II presiding over his royal court. The king gave the final verdict on the advice of nobles and church officials.

Women's rights

An unmarried woman had most of the same rights as a man, but a married woman could not own property without her husband's consent. Nor could a married woman be accused of a crime. A woman's husband was held responsible for any crimes she committed.

Trial by ordeal

Until about 1300, a person accused of a crime might be tried by ordeal.

- In one such trial, the accused person had to hold a red-hot metal bar in his bare hands.
- In another, the accused had to pick a stone out of a pan of boiling water.
- If the person's skin burned, he was found guilty. If it was not burned, he was declared innocent.

Nobles Rebel

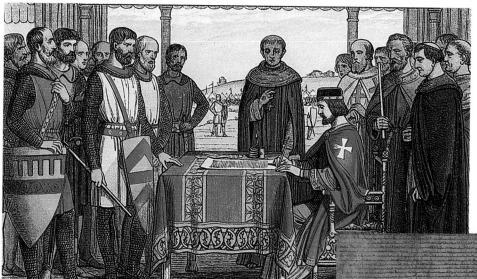

King John signed Magna Carta in 1215. The barons forced the king to act within the law of the land.

Despite their oaths of loyalty, lords sometimes rebelled against their king.

King John

When John became king of England in 1199, he misused his power. He demanded more military service from the lords, and sold royal positions to the highest bidder. He also raised taxes without the agreement of his nobles, known as barons.

The angry barons joined with the leaders of the church to demand that John meet them, and agree to a list of their rights. After the barons raised an army to back up their demands, King John met them at Runnymede, a meadow near the River Thames southwest of London.

Magna Carta

The barons forced the king to sign an agreement known as Magna Carta, which is Latin for "Great Charter." By signing it, the king promised to uphold feudal law, the old established laws of the land.

Most of the charter benefited the barons. Parts of it granted the church freedom from the king's interference,

Part of Magna Carta. There are four copies of the Great Charter in England. Two are in the British Library in London, one in Salisbury Cathedral, and one in Lincoln Cathedral.

Lost in the Wash

King John was not a lucky king. He is said to have lost all his treasure while crossing The Wash, a shallow bay on the east coast of England. He was marching to battle and lost his baggage train, with all his jewels, in a quicksand. According to another story, King John died soon afterwards – after eating too many fish.

and a few articles guaranteed the rights of the rising middle classes, such as town merchants. But ordinary people were hardly mentioned.

Magna Carta did not end the struggle between King John and the barons, however. A war broke out, and John died during the fighting. Later, Magna Carta came to be recognized as part of the basic law of England and of other English-speaking nations.

Parliament grows

King John's son, Henry III, also had trouble with the barons. A baron named Simon de Montfort led a rebellion against him. De Montfort was the first lord to summon ordinary English citizens to discuss government matters with the barons and church leaders. This led to the growth of Parliament. Simon de Montfort's revolt ended when he was killed in battle in 1265, but the king was never again to rule unchallenged.

Warwick Castle. English barons showed their power by building castles. Warwick town was fortified in the 900's, and later William the Conqueror built a castle there. From strong castles like Warwick, some barons dared to challenge their king.

Why Magna Carta was important

- Magna Carta ruled that the king must ask his barons for their advice and agreement in all matters important to the kingdom.

- Later, some parts of Magna Carta were used to declare that no law could be made without the consent, or agreement, of Parliament – the lawmaking body that represents all the people.

- Other parts of Magna Carta became the foundation for modern justice in many countries.

- One article in Magna Carta says that no freeman shall be imprisoned, deprived of property, sent out of the country, or destroyed except by the lawful judgment of his peers (equals) or by the law of the land.

31

Attacking a Castle

A siege was one way to attack a castle. A siege was a battle of wits and endurance between the attackers and the castle's defenders.

A siege during the wars of the 1400's between England and France. Joan of Arc leads French soldiers attacking a castle defended by the English.

No surprise

When an army marched to attack a castle, the defenders usually had plenty of warning. First, riders galloped in with news of the enemy's approach, and soon the dust of marching soldiers and horses was seen. Local people ran into the castle for shelter, bringing their pigs and cattle with them. Then the castle's huge gates were shut, and the bridge across the moat was pulled up by ropes or chains. Soldiers lined up behind the castle walls, ready to fight.

An army usually tried to capture a castle in two ways. First the soldiers tried to break through the walls. If that failed, they surrounded the castle and tried to force the defenders to surrender by starving them.

Attacking the walls

The attackers set up camp outside the castle. They tried to make holes in the castle walls by firing heavy stones from

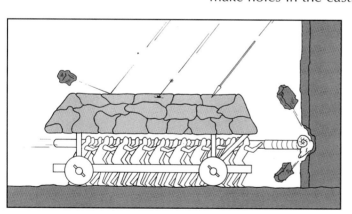

Battering rams pounded holes in castle gates. Some battering rams were mounted on wheels. They had leather-covered roofs to protect the men who pushed them up to the gates.

catapults or from primitive cannon. They dug tunnels under the castle walls to weaken them. They used battering rams to break down wooden gates. Some soldiers climbed ladders onto the wall. Others approached the castle inside wooden towers on wheels that were pushed up against the castle wall. Inside these siege towers, soldiers were protected from arrows and spears until they were close enough to fight the defenders on the castle wall.

Defending the walls

Soldiers inside the castle fired arrows out of narrow slits in the walls, and dropped stones onto the enemy. They often filled tubs with hot water or burning oil and poured it onto

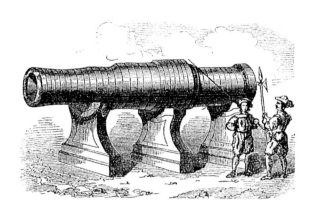

Cannon were first used in the 1300's. These huge guns fired heavy stone balls that could smash holes in castle walls.

Catapults were often used to attack castles and walled cities. The catapult worked like a giant slingshot to hurl heavy stones.

the attackers. They pushed away the enemy's ladders with long poles, and tried to set fire to their wooden siege towers.

With plenty of food and water inside the castle, the defenders had a good chance of winning. The attackers often gave up and left after a week or so. But if the siege lasted months – or even years – the defenders eventually ran out of food or grew weak with sickness. Then they had to surrender and open the castle gates.

A castle on a hill was hard to attack. A massive castle built in the 1400's stands on the Rock of Cashel, or Castle Rock, in Tipperary, Ireland. There was a fortress here as early as the 500's.

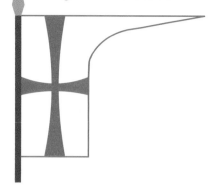

Knights on Crusade

The Crusades were military expeditions by Christians from Europe to Palestine, known as the Holy Land. Knights from all over Europe fought in these holy wars.

The crusaders' flag bore a red cross. The word Crusade comes from the Latin word *crux*, meaning cross.

Aims of the Crusades

Christian pilgrims from Europe journeyed to the city of Jerusalem and other holy places in Palestine where Jesus Christ had lived. In the 600's, Arab Muslims gained control of Jerusalem, but they still let Christians visit the city. Then, during the 1000's, Seljuk Turks from central Asia conquered Palestine. They were Muslims too, but unlike the Arabs, they made it difficult for Christians to visit the holy places.

A crusader castle – the Krak des Chevaliers – still stands in Syria. It was built in the 1100's by the Knights Hospitallers, a famous order of knights. The castle, which was big enough to house several thousand knights, withstood many attacks. It was captured only by a trick when the Muslims sent in a fake letter that persuaded the crusaders to surrender.

A holy lance

The First Crusade of 1096 included French and Norman knights. There were also soldiers from the Byzantine Empire, the old eastern Roman Empire. Its capital was Constantinople (old Byzantium; now Istanbul, Turkey).

- The crusaders captured Antioch, in northern Syria, after a long siege.

- Many knights died in battle or from hunger. Others went home.

- After they captured the city, the crusaders were attacked by the Turks.

- The crusaders were exhausted, but the discovery of a lance said to have wounded Jesus on the cross inspired them to victory.

- In 1099, after six weeks of fighting, they took the city of Jerusalem.

Pope Innocent III, head of the Catholic Church, persuaded many French knights to join the Fourth Crusade in 1202. This Crusade failed. First, the crusaders went off to help the rulers of Venice attack a city in what is now Croatia. Then they attacked Constantinople to put a new ruler on the throne of the Byzantine Empire. They never got to the Holy Land.

The Children's Crusade

In 1212 thousands of poor boys and girls became convinced that God would help them recover Jerusalem. Two groups set out, from France and Germany, but none of the children reached the Holy Land. Some died during the long journey across Europe to the Mediterranean Sea. Those who reached the sea expected its waters to part so that they could cross safely to Jerusalem. When no such miracle took place, some children returned home. Others boarded ships, and were either drowned in storms or sold into slavery.

The crusaders then decided to fight for the Holy Land. Armies of knights and other soldiers traveled over land and sea from Europe to Palestine. Many wore a cross, like the cross of Christ, on their clothing, but not all crusaders joined the expeditions for religious reasons. Some wanted land or trade and others sought adventure and riches.

The Crusades end

The First Crusade set out in 1096, and captured Jerusalem in 1099, but the wars went on for many years. In 1187 the Muslim leader Saladin recaptured Jerusalem. He agreed to let Christian pilgrims visit freely, but still the crusaders fought to gain Jerusalem. The Eighth and last Crusade took place in 1270. After that, Europeans made no further serious efforts to capture the Holy Land.

A Muslim pharmacist prepares a drug. Crusaders saw new ways of life in the East, and found the Arabs were more advanced in science and medicine than Europeans. For many years before the Crusades, there had been trade between Muslims and Europeans. The cities of Constantinople and Venice were important links between East and West. The Crusades helped develop such contacts.

The Seventh Crusade (1248-1254) was led by King Louis IX of France (Saint Louis). This painting from the 1400's shows him with his army at the start of the long journey. Louis was captured by the Muslims, who freed him on payment of a huge ransom. Louis also led the Eighth – and last – Crusade in 1270 but he became ill and died when disease broke out among his troops.

35

The Church

The Christian Church was powerful in the Middle Ages. After the fall of the Roman Empire, the church in Rome became a unifying force in western Europe.

A divided church

The two main Christian churches were the Catholic Church in Rome and the Eastern Orthodox Church in Constantinople. The two split in 1054 after a disagreement over the authority of the pope, the head of the church.

The monks of Saint Benedict

Benedict was born in Norcia, Italy, about 480. He lived alone in a cave, and his simple religious way of life attracted others to follow his example. He established small communities of monks and drew up a rule (a set of guidelines) for them to follow. These guidelines were followed by most monks from the 800's on. Benedictine monks lived together in buildings known as monasteries.

Wandering friars

Monasteries became centers of learning, and monks spent much time in prayer and religious worship. New religious orders, whose members were called friars, were founded in the 1200's. Franciscan friars followed the example of Saint Francis of Assisi. They lived simply and wandered from place to place, preaching and caring for people. The Dominican friars, founded in 1216 by Saint Dominic, became noted for their scholarship.

King, knights, and archbishop

In 1162 Thomas Becket was made archbishop of Canterbury, head of the church in England, by his friend King Henry II. But when Henry tried to limit the powers of the church, Becket resisted. This made the king angry and Henry asked – in the hearing of his knights – if anyone was brave enough to rid him of a single troublesome priest. Four knights took the king's remark as a royal request and killed Becket in Canterbury Cathedral. The pope declared Becket a saint in 1173, and many pilgrims came to visit his tomb at Canterbury.

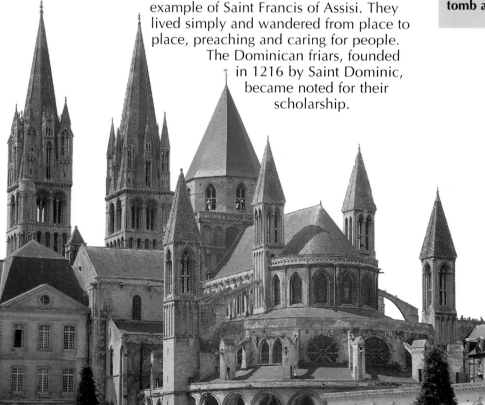

A large church in Caen, France, built in the Romanesque style. This style of architecture reached its peak in Europe during the 1000's and 1100's.

The pope

The pope in Rome, Italy, was the head of the church in western Europe. Powerful popes such as Innocent III (reigned 1198-1216) had great influence in political affairs. Sometimes popes quarreled with kings. By 1100, the popes claimed the power to remove a king if they disapproved of him. In 1303 Pope Boniface VIII was held prisoner by French soldiers after a quarrel with the king of France. Between 1379 and 1417 there were two rival popes – one in Avignon, France, and the other in Rome. There was even more confusion when a third pope was chosen for a short time. These disagreements weakened the power of the church.

Stained glass windows in churches often illustrated stories from the Bible in sparkling light and glowing colors. Few people could read, so the scenes helped teach Bible stories.

FACTS ABOUT MONASTERIES

- The first monasteries were probably founded in Ireland between A.D. 432 and 463 by Saint Patrick, who converted the Irish people to Christianity.

- Monks educated children and cared for the sick.

- Some monks observed a rule of silence, rarely speaking.

- The Cistercians, an order of monks, developed an excellent breed of sheep and encouraged sheep-farming.

- Benedictine monks in France made an alcoholic drink, which is named after them.

Building a cathedral was a huge undertaking. When a town wanted to build a new cathedral, the townspeople labored alongside skilled workers such as stonemasons and makers of stained glass. This picture of the 1400's shows builders at work.

Art and Books

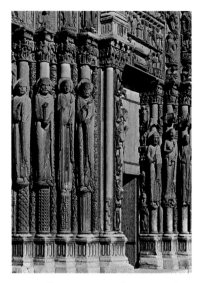

Stone figures were often carved on the walls of buildings, as seen here on Chartres Cathedral in France.

The pictures of the Middle Ages often look different from those of later times. Books too were different – and very valuable.

Purple heaven

Artists in the Middle Ages painted mainly religious subjects. In these pictures, they made no attempt to show the world as it really was, and the pictures they painted often have a flat look. Artists used special colors or styles as symbols. For example, a sky painted gold or purple symbolized God's kingdom in heaven. Artists painted pictures called frescoes on the walls of churches.

In the late 1200's, a few artists in Europe began to paint people and scenes in a more lifelike way. The greatest of these new painters was an Italian named Giotto. He painted people who looked real, with expressions that showed their feelings.

Books and writers

Most people were unable to read or write in those days, and few people owned books. If a person wanted to send a letter, he hired a professional writer called a scribe to write the letter for him. Monks in monasteries copied books by hand. These books were written in Latin. They were called manuscripts, and many were illuminated, or decorated with designs and pictures on each page.

Why are very old books hard to read?

C ȝ g

A.D. 300   800   today

Old manuscripts are hard to read because the letters look different from those we use today. The small letter g appeared in the 300's. Monks who copied books by hand reshaped the letter in the 800's, and by about 1500 the letter looked as it does today. Other letters of the alphabet changed over time in the same way.

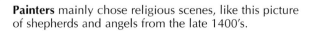

Painters mainly chose religious scenes, like this picture of shepherds and angels from the late 1400's.

By the 1300's, European authors were writing books in their own languages. Dante Alighieri wrote a long religious poem called *The Divine Comedy* in Italian. In England, Geoffrey Chaucer wrote *The Canterbury Tales* in English. The invention of printing with movable type in the mid-1400's made it possible for books to be produced cheaply and in large numbers for the first time.

Geoffrey Chaucer was a famous English writer of the Middle Ages. This picture of Chaucer on horseback comes from a copy of his *Canterbury Tales*, dating from 1400 to 1410. The page is beautifully decorated and handwritten.

What were gargoyles?

Gargoyles were practical as well as decorative. Builders of the Middle Ages made these waterspouts so that rainwater running off the roof was kept away from the walls. Water ran through a hollow channel inside the gargoyle, and gushed out of its mouth. The gargoyles were often fantastic figures, part-animal and part-human.

Artists and builders worked together to build cathedrals. Waterspouts called gargoyles (left) were added to such buildings. Inside Amiens Cathedral in France (right), a high, arched ceiling is supported by massive stone pillars. The Amiens Cathedral was begun in the 1200's.

Legends and Stories

Stories about King Arthur's knights told how they looked for the Holy Grail. This 19th-century tapestry by the artist Sir Edward Burne-Jones shows Sir Perceval (right), one of the knights, kneeling before the Grail.

Sir Lancelot was one of Arthur's bravest knights. He too sought the Holy Grail. This picture made in France about 1300 shows Lancelot with his horse. On his quest, he is meeting with a hermit, or holy man, in a tree house.

Storytellers

People have always enjoyed listening to and telling stories. In olden times, stories and legends were handed down by word of mouth. They were told around the fire in the Great Hall of the castle, and by the villagers in their homes. Wandering minstrels came to entertain the lord in his castle with stories of adventure and daring deeds. Singers called troubadours also composed love songs for noblemen and ladies. They told tales of noble kings, gallant knights, and fair ladies. Some real-life knights made up stories of their own, and exaggerated their adventures.

The legend of King Arthur

Stories of King Arthur told how he led a band of Christian knights, including Lancelot and Galahad. In their many adventures, they faced great perils while searching for the Holy Grail. According to the legend, the Holy Grail was the cup used by Jesus Christ at the Last Supper before he was crucified. Arthur and his knights met around a round table. They protected the weak against the wicked and were often guided in their adventures by true love of a lady.

Was there a real King Arthur?

We do not know. He may have been a British leader who fought German invaders when they came to Britain about A.D. 500, as the Romans left. Storytellers passed on the early tales about Arthur by word of mouth. A Welshman named Geoffrey of Monmouth wrote the stories down about 1150, and they were then told and retold by other writers across western Europe.

Robin Hood

Robin Hood was a legendary English outlaw who stole from the rich and gave to the poor. Many stories told of his daring, and he became a folk hero. According to the stories, Robin Hood and his followers lived in Sherwood Forest, near Nottingham, in the 1100's. Among Robin's companions were Friar Tuck, a fat, jolly priest; Little John, a giant of a man; and Maid Marian, Robin's sweetheart. In their adventures, the outlaws outwitted their enemies – the cruel Sheriff of Nottingham and bad King John. These tales were first written down in the late 1400's, but people told stories about Robin Hood long before that.

Robin Hood and his outlaws were famous for their skill with bows and arrows. Their green clothing helped them hide among the trees of Sherwood Forest, where they lived. Robin Hood was seen as a hero of the common people against the unjust King John.

William Tell prepares to shoot the apple off his son's head.

William Tell

William Tell was a legendary hero of Switzerland. He represented the spirit of the Swiss as they struggled for independence from Austrian rule in the 1300's. The story tells how the Austrian governor of Tell's canton (state) set a hat on a pole in the town square and ordered every Swiss to bow to it. When William Tell refused, he was arrested. The governor promised to free him if he could shoot an arrow off his own son's head. Tell, famous for his skill with a crossbow, did exactly that. But the promise was not kept and Tell remained a prisoner. He eventually escaped, killed the governor, and led a revolt against the Austrians.

The Canterbury Tales

The Canterbury Tales are stories written in verse by Geoffrey Chaucer, who lived from about 1340 to 1400. Chaucer was the greatest English poet of the Middle Ages – a learned man who traveled in Europe on diplomatic missions and wrote for people at the court of the king. In *The Canterbury Tales*, he tells of a group of pilgrims traveling from London to the shrine of Saint Thomas Becket at Canterbury. On their journey, each pilgrim tells a tale to entertain the others.

Chaucer's pilgrims on the road to Canterbury. They include a knight, a parson, a plowman, a nun, and a miller – men and women from different walks of life sharing their stories on the four-day journey from London. This illustration was made in the 1400's.

Learning and Knowledge

Many scholars and teachers were monks or priests. Few ordinary people even went to school. From the 1100's, universities became new centers of learning, but in the face of a disaster like the Black Death, everyone was helpless.

Making books

Until the 1300's, books were always written in Latin. This had been the language of the Romans, and was understood by educated people throughout Europe. It was also the language used in church. Only young men who were to become monks or priests received proper schooling.

Books were made by monks. One group of monks made the parchment pages and another group of monks wrote the letters. A third group of monks did the illumination. These colored decorations included animals, human figures, branches with leaves, geometric designs, and ornamental letters. A fourth group of monks bound the finished pages into books.

Monks copied out books by hand, and decorated the pages. Every copy of a book took many hours to make. Monks in monasteries throughout Europe helped preserve the writings of the ancient Greeks and Romans.

Scholars at the University of Paris. The first universities founded in Europe were at Bologna, Italy (about 1100), and Paris, France (late 1100's). Universities developed gradually from groups of separate schools.

Easier reading

The old Latin writing of Roman times used only capital letters and ran all the words together. In the Middle Ages, scribes developed a system of writing that was easier to read than Roman writing.

- They used capital letters and small letters.
- They set up a system of punctuation.
- They left spaces between words.

The Book of Kells is an illuminated manuscript of the Gospels (part of the Bible). It was made in Ireland between the mid-700's and early 800's.

Easier adding

The Romans wrote I II III IV V VI VII VIII IX X

In the Hindu-Arabic system, people wrote
   1 2 3 4 5 6 7 8 9 10

- The Hindus of India also invented the zero (0), which the Romans never used.
- The Arabs learned the Hindu system during the 700's.
- In the 1100's a book written by a Persian mathematician in the 800's was translated into Latin.
- In this way, the numerals we use today first reached Europe.

Universities

Students at university studied only certain subjects. These included spoken and written Latin, arithmetic (using Roman numbers), geometry, astronomy, and music. New subjects were added when Muslim scholars from North Africa and Moorish Spain brought long-lost Greek and Roman scholarship to Europe. Muslim scholars brought another important change, too. They introduced the Hindu-Arabic number system to Europe, and this made it easier to do calculations, especially in business. The University of Paris became a model for other universities, including – from the 1200's – Oxford and Cambridge in England.

The Black Death

Doctors in Europe knew little about how the human body worked. They based treatments on traditional

The Black Death caused fear and panic across Europe. This disease killed millions of people, and doctors could do little to help. Here, people are burning the possessions of victims to prevent the disease from spreading.

A doctor bandages a broken jaw. Doctors knew little about medical science and relied on a mixture of magic and folk remedies, such as herb medicines.

methods, and were helpless against a terrible disease that struck in the 1300's. This was a form of bubonic plague that killed about one-fourth of Europe's population. The disease was named the Black Death because its victims developed black spots beneath the skin. It was passed to humans mainly by fleas from infected rats.

Between 1334 and 1352, the Black Death swept across China, India, Persia, Russia, Italy, France, England, Germany, and Norway. People fleeing from towns to escape the disease took it to the countryside. Whole villages were wiped out. Some people said the Black Death was God's punishment for human wickedness. Yet in a few years, the disease had passed, and Europe was recovering.

Leisure and Play

King John of England, like most kings, enjoyed hunting. This picture from the early 1300's shows the king chasing a deer with his hounds. Deer meat, or venison, was often served in noble households. The poor were not allowed to hunt deer.

In the Great Hall of the castle, the lord and his knights ate, drank, and played gambling games, such as dice. Outdoors, they entertained themselves by training for war. Knights fought mock-battles and hunted wild animals.

War games

A knight spent much of his time exercising and training. He had to keep his body fit and strong to use heavy weapons such as the sword and mace (a kind of club). Knights sometimes took part in jousts. In these contests, two knights – on horseback and in full armor – charged at one another. Each man tried to hit the other with his lance and knock him to the ground. The lances were usually fitted with blunt tips to prevent serious injury, but some knights fought to the death.

Groups of knights took part in other mock-battles which sometimes became so lifelike that men were seriously wounded or killed. Crowds of people gathered to watch these fights, as well as the archery contests and wrestling bouts that took place at the same time.

Hunting

Lords and ladies enjoyed hunting. They rode into the forests with packs of hunting dogs to chase deer, wild boar, and other wild animals. Kings often set aside huge areas of land for their own private hunting parks. Another popular sport was hawking. In hawking, birds of prey such as hawks and falcons were trained to catch hares, and birds such as pigeons or ducks.

Miracles and farces

Some dramas of the Middle Ages were called miracle plays and morality plays.

- Miracle plays told stories from the lives of the saints or the Virgin Mary.

- Morality plays used a story to teach a moral lesson.

- In time, professional actors began to perform plays.

- Some actors became part of noble households. They entertained guests with folk tales and comic skits between courses at banquets.

- These entertainments were called farces and interludes.

A French tapestry made in the late 1400's is called *The Unicorn at the Fountain*. The people surrounding the animals are nobles and huntsmen. The detail (right) shows two hunting dogs.

Ladies at home

The lord's wife was expected to sew, spin, and weave, and to rule the household servants, but her main responsibility was to give birth to male children. If she did not have at least one son, her husband could end the marriage. Some noblewomen took part in outdoor pursuits, such as hunting. Others passed their time making tapestry pictures woven from colored threads.

Watching a play

There were no theaters as we know them today. In the early Middle Ages, religious plays were performed in church. From the 1200's plays were moved outdoors. The dramas of this time are often called "mystery" plays. Performances of these plays were then taken over by townspeople who were members of guilds (trade associations), such as bakers, weavers, and silversmiths. They paid for the productions, and acted in the plays.

In England, the setting for each play was mounted on a cart called a pageant wagon. The wagon was drawn through the city and stopped at various places, where the audience gathered to enjoy the performance.

Pageant wagons were stages on wheels. The audience watched the play in the street or from nearby houses. The actors were townspeople.

45

The chain dance, popular in the Middle Ages, was a peasant dance, later taken up by the nobles. People danced to celebrate weddings, holidays, and other festive occasions.

In their free time, people enjoyed sports and pastimes, such as outdoor and indoor games, music, and dancing.

Indoor pastimes

Noblemen and women played board games such as chess and backgammon. Dice games were often played for money. Music, singing, and dancing were popular with rich and poor alike. Folk dances enjoyed by peasants included chain dances and dance games, such as ring-a-ring o' roses. Nobles developed more elegant versions of these village dances. For example, they performed the carol, a circle dance, in a slower and more dignified manner than the lively style of the peasants.

Professional dancers, jugglers, acrobats, and animal trainers wandered from town to town, performing in the town square or on the village green. Dancing was also a popular part of the religious plays performed by the guilds.

Troubadours and minstrels

Most music was performed in church before 900. Later, French nobles made up songs and poems that were not religious. These poet-composers were the first troubadours. In Germany, similar performers were called minnesingers. Their songs often told of a knight's hopeless love for a lady of high social position.

Only men and boys sang in church choirs. This marble relief sculpture made in 1431 shows boys singing a psalm.

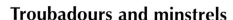

Minstrels make merry

At the marriage of Princess Margaret of England in 1290, it is said that 426 minstrels were hired to entertain the guests.

King Edward I's many court minstrels included two women, who performed under the names of Matill Makejoye and Pearl in the Egg!

Professional entertainers such as these were also known as minstrels. A minstrel might be a musician, singer, storyteller, juggler, tumbler (acrobat), or clown. Storytellers also traveled around the countryside, gathering news and passing on stories from one region to another. There were no newspapers in those days, so a traveling entertainer had much to tell as he rested at the local inn, and chatted to the villagers. A troubadour knew all the latest gossip and scandals at court. He was expected to compose verses at a moment's notice, and to play at least two musical instruments.

Jesters

At court, a king often had a jester or fool whose job was to tell jokes, act the fool, and generally amuse his master. The jester wore a cap with bells. At court banquets he would sometimes make fun of guests, who had to laugh in spite of their own discomfort – or risk angering the king.

Minstrels visited castles to entertain lords, ladies, and servants with long songs about the heroic deeds of legendary kings and knights. The musician (left) in this picture from the 1300's is playing a stringed instrument similar to a violin.

A knight playing chess. Chess, played in Europe from the 1000's, was popular among nobles.

Dance of death

During the Black Death in the 1300's, people sang and danced frantically in graveyards. They believed this would drive away evil demons, and keep them safe from the disease. Some people danced wildly through the streets until they fainted – or dropped dead.

Fashion and Dress

Ordinary people wore simple clothing made of cloth, animal fur, and leather. They made their own clothes at home, using wool from sheep and linen from flax plants. They spun thread on spinning wheels, and wove it into fabric on looms. Rich people paid tailors to make clothes that were often costly and fancy.

A knight's clothes

Beneath his armor, a knight wore long stockings and a tunic that reached to his knees. This shirtlike garment had sleeves and was made of linen or wool. Over this tunic, the knight wore a sleeveless tunic open at the sides and fastened with a belt. His cloak fastened at the shoulders.

More elegant wear

Women of the early Middle Ages wore simple, loose tunics. Later, they wore long dresses that were laced to fit the upper part of the body. Men wore loose breeches (trouserlike garments) under their tunics. Some men wore long, brightly colored stockings, while others wrapped long strips of cloth around their legs.

   The growing towns now had shops run by weavers, tailors, shoemakers, and other craftworkers. They began to cut, fit, and decorate clothes with more skill for wealthy customers.

A woman wearing a hennin. A hennin was a high, cone-shaped headdress worn from the 1400's.

A woman's hairstyle of the 1400's is shown in this Italian painting. She has plucked or shaved her hair at the front to make her forehead seem higher. Blond hair was very fashionable too.

What were hairstyles like?

- Most men wore their hair shoulder-length.
- Priests and monks had a shaved patch called a tonsure on the crown of their head.
- Girls and unmarried women wore their hair loose. Married women covered their hair with a veil or a hoodlike covering.
- Some women plucked or shaved their hair at the front to make their forehead seem higher – a sign of beauty.

High and wide

Women wore elaborate headdresses. The hennin rose about 36 inches (90 centimeters) high and was draped with a veil. Men wore a draped turban called a chaperon.

Men also wore pointed-toe shoes called poulanes. On some shoes the points measured 6 inches (15 centimeters) or more.

Animal furs were used to trim clothing: ermine, marten, and sable for court lords and ladies; fox, otter, and rabbit for lesser nobility and the middle classes.

Builders in the 1200's wear the working clothes of the time – a simple tunic and breeches, and cloth cap. The crane (right) is powered by a man walking on the steps of a large wheel, or treadmill.

Changes in fashion

During the 1100's and 1200's, women wore metal hairnets, veils, and draped throat covers called wimples. Men wore hoods that had long tails. Both men and women wore outer tunics or surcoats, which were sometimes ankle-length.

By the 1300's the fashion had changed. Men's surcoats were now hip-length, and buttoned down the front. A rich man's clothes might have dozens of buttons, and his jacket was fastened with a belt studded with jewels. On his head, he wore a felt hat decorated with jewels.

In the 1400's the surcoat was pleated, edged with fur, and fastened at the waist by a belt. The shoulders were padded and the chest stiffened to make the wearer's waist appear smaller. By now, men's shoes had become so pointed that the front was often curled up and fastened to the knee with a small chain!

The wimple was a throat cover worn by women in Europe during the 1200's, usually with various hoodlike head coverings.

This Italian painting shows men and women at a wedding. The women wear long trailing gowns and tall headdresses. The men wear short tunics, capes, and fancy hats.

Cities and Trade

People in the Middle Ages did not shop as often as we do now. They probably went to market once a month. Some big markets were held once a year. These trade fairs helped encourage the growth of busy cities.

To market

Farmers went to market to buy and sell animals, and to sell food when they had more than enough for themselves. Other people might buy clay pots, a new knife, or a length of rope. People enjoyed going to market to meet old friends, gossip, and hear news of the world beyond the village.

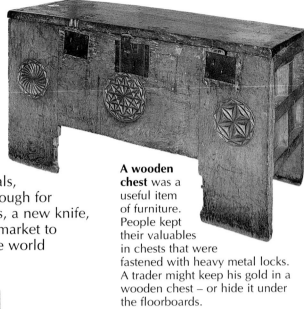

A wooden chest was a useful item of furniture. People kept their valuables in chests that were fastened with heavy metal locks. A trader might keep his gold in a wooden chest – or hide it under the floorboards.

Banks

As trade grew, so did the need for a better money system. Merchants had been accustomed to carrying gold around with them to pay for what they bought. But gold was heavy to carry, and easy to steal. It was safer to have a bank handle your money. Banks were started to save merchants from carrying heavy sacks of gold with them on their business trips.

DID YOU KNOW?

Modern banking began between the 1200's and 1600's in Italy. The word bank comes from the Italian word *banco* or *banca*, meaning bench. Early Italian bankers did business on benches in the street.

A banker in the Middle Ages pays out money to a customer.

Trade fairs

The most popular markets grew into trade fairs. These fairs were held each year in certain cities, and merchants from all over Europe – and beyond – came to buy and sell goods. They also exchanged ideas with other merchants about new products and production methods. Trade between different parts of Europe grew during the Middle Ages, helping to spread prosperity and knowledge.

Trading towns and ports grew into larger cities. Merchants in Flanders (now part of Belgium) flourished and Flanders became one of the busiest marketplaces in Europe. It was an important center for the wool trade with England across the North Sea, and with other European countries.

At a trade fair, a bishop is blessing the traders, who seem more interested in discussing prices. A shepherd has driven a flock of sheep (bottom right) to be sold. Some buildings have signs hanging outside that show what is for sale inside.

Going to Sea

Merchants and traders, as well as explorers, went to sea in wooden sailing ships. Most sailors stayed close to shore, but some made daring voyages in search of new lands.

Viking long ships

Among the bravest sailors of the Middle Ages were the Vikings. They came from the lands of Scandinavia that are now Denmark, Norway, and Sweden. The Vikings built long wooden ships powered by oars and a single sail. A Viking ship sailed well in rough seas or calm waters, and was light enough to enter shallow rivers. Some of these ships had as many as 30 oars on each side. There were trading ships carrying goods, families, and farm animals to new lands. There were also warships, called long ships, in which bands of warriors set out to raid and plunder.

Viking ships were the best in northern Europe between the A.D. 700's and the late 1000's. Bold Vikings sailed their ships across the Atlantic Ocean to Greenland and North America.

Ships for trade and war

As trade by sea increased, merchants needed roomier ships to carry more cargo. By about 1200, shipbuilders in northern Europe had developed a new and sturdy ship called the cog. A cog was wider and deeper than a Viking long ship. It could carry goods such as wool or wine, or it could carry soldiers. The cog had two raised wooden structures called castles – one at the front, and one at the stern. The forecastle at the front was a platform from which soldiers could fire arrows and stones at enemy ships. The sterncastle was a shelter for important passengers. Ordinary sailors lived, ate, and slept on deck.

Following the raven

The Viking flag showed a raven – a bird of special importance to these brave adventurers.

● In Norse myth, the god Odin had two sacred ravens that flew about the world each day and returned at night to tell all they had seen.

● Viking sailors took ravens with them on ocean voyages because the birds were known for their ability to find land.

● If sailors were unsure where land lay, they released a raven from the ship and then sailed in the direction that the bird flew.

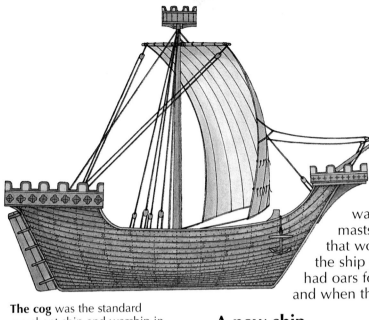

The cog was the standard merchant ship and warship in northern Europe from about 1200 to the mid-1400's. Like the Viking ship, it had one large sail.

Galleys

On the Mediterranean Sea, people sailed in oared ships called galleys. Galleys had been used in the Mediterranean for hundreds of years, as cargo and passenger ships as well as warships. They had two or even three masts, and triangular sails called lateens that worked better than square sails when the ship was sailing into the wind. Galleys had oars for use when there was no wind, and when the ship was entering or leaving port.

A new ship

About the mid-1400's, shipbuilders combined the best features of the cog and the Mediterranean galley. They produced a new sailing ship with both square and lateen sails. This ship was called a carrack, and its basic design remained unchanged for the next 300 years.

How did sailors find their way?

Sailors took sightings of the sun and stars to find out where they were at sea. They also relied on landmarks such as cliffs or islands.

● By the 1100's, sailors were using magnetic compasses. The first compasses were simply pieces of magnetic iron floated on straw or cork in a bowl of water. The iron turned to point north.

● By the 1300's, compasses had a card marked off into 32 points of direction.

How were ships steered?

A Viking ship was steered by a long oar at the stern. The cog was steered by a wooden rudder. The Chinese were the first people to use the rudder, and this invention reached Europe by about 1200.

A Norman army crossed the sea from France to conquer England in 1066. This picture, from the Bayeux Tapestry, shows the invasion fleet at sea. Each ship has one mast with a big sail, and is steered by a large oar at the stern.

Famous People

The lives of four very different people show what brought lasting fame in the age of knights and castles.

Charlemagne or Charles the Great, born in 742, was the most famous ruler of the Middle Ages. He was king of the Franks, but conquered most of western Europe, including what are now Belgium, France, Luxembourg, and the Netherlands, as well as most of Germany and Italy. On Christmas Day, 800, Charlemagne was crowned emperor of the Romans. This led to the birth of the Holy Roman Empire, which lasted in some form until 1806.

Charlemagne was a wise ruler. At his palace he set up a school for priests and scholars from all over his empire. This school trained teachers for other places of learning throughout Europe. Scholars at the schools collected and copied ancient Roman writings which otherwise would have been lost.

Charlemagne. This statue in silver and gold, encrusted with emeralds and rubies, was made about 1349. It stands in the cathedral at Aachen (Germany), Charlemagne's capital.

Saint Francis, in this painting by the Italian artist Giovanni Bellini, stands outside a simple dwelling with some of the animals he loved.

Saint Francis of Assisi was one of the most popular saints of the Middle Ages. Francis was born about 1181 in Assisi, a small town in Italy. In 1205 Francis believed he heard a call from God to repair a ruined church near Assisi. He turned away from his wealthy family and friends to live in poverty, preaching and healing the sick. Soon he attracted followers and founded the Franciscan order of friars, or traveling preachers. He died in 1226 and was made a saint two years later. Saint Francis is known as the saint who loved animals.

Marco Polo (in green) kneels with his father and uncle before Kublai Khan, the Mongol ruler of China (in blue). This picture shows the Chinese emperor dressed as a European.

Marco Polo was the most famous European traveler of the Middle Ages. He was born in Venice, Italy, in 1254. His father and uncle were merchants, and in 1271 they set out on an expedition to China. Marco Polo, aged 17, went with them.

In China they were welcomed by Emperor Kublai Khan, who sent Marco on many official tours around his huge empire. No European had seen so much of China before. The Polos began to think they would never return home. Finally they were allowed to escort a Chinese princess to her wedding in Persia. Then they made their way overland to Turkey, and from there to Venice.

The Polos arrived home in 1295, having been away for 24 years! Marco Polo wrote a book about his adventures. He told of the many marvels he had seen, such as how the Chinese used paper money (unknown in Europe).

Joan of Arc was burned at the stake by her captors in 1431.

Joan of Arc was a simple peasant girl who became the heroine of France. She was born about 1412, at a time when France was being defeated by England during the Hundred Years' War.

Like most peasants, Joan never learned to read or write, but she was deeply religious. At the age of 13 she began hearing what she believed were the voices of saints. These voices persuaded her that God had chosen her to help King Charles VII of France drive the English from French soil. She convinced the king to let her lead his soldiers and inspired the French to victory in several battles. Then, in 1430, she was captured by enemies who handed her over to the English. The English imprisoned her and accused her of being a witch. Joan insisted her visions and voices came from God, but she was burned at the stake in 1431. She was declared a saint by the Roman Catholic Church in 1920.

The Last Castles

Beaumaris Castle in north Wales was built for King Edward I of England in the 1200's. It is a good example of the concentric or ring castle that was especially difficult to capture. This type of castle owed much to the influence of crusaders, who had seen such castles in the East.

Bunratty Castle in County Clare, Ireland, has a massive box-shaped keep. It dates from the 1400's, when lords built castles as fortified homes.

Castles were built to last forever. But by the 1300's, the use of gunpowder in warfare meant that new styles of castles were needed. The gun, not the knight, now ruled the battlefield.

Castles with ring walls

Crusader knights who went from Europe to the Middle East brought back new ideas about castle-building. In the East they had seen castles with rings of walls at different levels. Inside the main wall were a second and a third wall. Huge new castles of this type, called concentric castles, were built from about 1270 in Britain. Most of the large castles built in Wales by King Edward I were concentric. The king hired an expert castle-builder, Master James of St. George, to plan his new castles. They were the finest fortresses of their time.

Deal Castle, in Kent, England, was built for King Henry VIII. It took only two years to build (1539-1540), much less time than earlier castles. This castle has six short turrets surrounding the central keep. Cannon mounted on the flat tops of the turrets could fire at ships.

Gunpowder

Gunpowder was first used in western Europe at the Battle of Crécy, in France, in 1346. This marked the start of a new age in warfare. Gunpowder could explode with enough power to shatter the walls of the strongest castle. Castles built after the mid-1300's reflect the change in fighting methods that followed the first use of this powerful new weapon.

Castles as homes

By the 1400's some castles were built of brick, not stone. They were strong and well defended. Some had openings in the walls through which cannon could be fired, but these castles were used as homes, not fortresses. The castle owner did not expect to fight off a siege or keep a company of armed knights.

Castles were still built, however. In the 1500's, Henry VIII of England had a series of new castles built to defend the southeast coast of England. These castles had guns that could fire at ships, and they had short turrets called bastions instead of tall towers.

The end of armor

The age of knights in armor was coming to an end. During the 1500's people wore armor mainly to take part in tournaments and ceremonial occasions. The Spanish soldiers who conquered the Aztecs of Mexico wore chest armor, but by the 1600's, few soldiers wore armor on the battlefield. It was too heavy, and could not protect them against handguns and cannon.

Castle and cannon

Very few castles could stand up to the pounding of heavy cannon. One castle that did was Corfe Castle in Dorset, England.

- **In the 1640's, during the English Civil War, this castle withstood a nine-month battering by the guns of Parliament's army.**

- **Oliver Cromwell was Parliament's leading general. His soldiers, known as Roundheads, fought the soldiers of King Charles I, known as Royalists or Cavaliers.**

- **Cromwell usually knocked down castles that had stood against him, so that they could not be used again.**

Castles Around the World

Many castles were built in Europe during the Middle Ages, but people in other parts of the world also built castles.

The Moors built castles in North Africa, and in the parts of Spain that they ruled. Portuguese traders who sailed to Africa built trading forts similar to castles along the African coast. People in Korea, Japan, and India also built castles.

Make way for elephants

Indian castles were much like those of Europe and the Middle East, though often more richly decorated. The gate of an Indian castle was also higher – high enough for an elephant to walk through!

In India, elephants were used in battles. Soldiers rode on elephants' backs, inside small wooden shelters that looked like miniature castles. An elephant could break down the wooden doors of a castle just by pushing against them with its head. To prevent this, castle doors usually had long iron spikes sticking out from the wood.

North African castles have changed little over the centuries. Taourit Kasbah, a castle in Morocco, looks ancient but was built in the 1930's, in the style of earlier North African castles.

Jaisalmer Fort in Rajasthan, India, built in 1156. Like castles in Europe, it has stone walls with towers. Local rulers in India built castles as symbols of their power.

Castles of Japan

The Japanese began to build stone castles in the late 1500's. These castles were tall buildings, surrounded by water-filled moats. The castle stood on a stone base, but the upper walls were made of wood and plaster, and were not strong enough to stand up to artillery. This did not matter greatly. When these castles were built, there were few cannon in Japan. Most battles were fought on open ground between armies of samurai warriors.

The samurai were knights. They wore armor, and their main weapons were curved swords, and bows and arrows. They were proud of their ancient traditions and bound by a code of loyalty to their lords, who were called daimyos. The samurai were graded in military ranks, each rank being paid an appropriate amount in rice.

Osaka Castle stands on a hill in the city of Osaka, Japan. It was completed in 1586.

Fortress of the Incas

About 1520, the Incas built a massive fortress beside their royal city of Cusco in Peru. It was called Sacsahuaman.

- Some of its stones weigh 100 tons (91 metric tons).

- The builders set these huge stones together without using cement.

- They cut and shaped each stone to fit against the others, like pieces of a giant jigsaw puzzle.

- When Spanish soldiers conquered Cusco, they used stones from the fortress to build houses.

59

Castles Today

People enjoy visiting castles. In some castles, we may admire works of art, suits of armor, and old weapons. In others, we can peer into dark, grim dungeons or prison cells. Castles are now among the top tourist attractions in the world.

Pretend castles

From the 1700's, architects in Europe began copying the styles of the Middle Ages to build mock-castles. These looked like old castles, but were not meant for warfare at all. Wealthy people chose to live in mansions that looked like Scottish fortresses or French castles. Some rich people even had ruined castles built in the parks of their country houses, because they liked to have an interesting jumble of stones to look at and walk around.

Mock-battles entertain visitors to Bruges in Belgium. They enjoy watching knights jousting during a pageant that brings the Middle Ages to life. The knights represent two noble families who first fought in this tournament in 1392.

Two fairytale castles. Neuschwanstein Castle (left) is in Bavaria, Germany. It looks like a castle that knights might have lived in, but was actually built in 1869. It was built for King Ludwig II of Bavaria, who was known as Mad King Ludwig. The king's castle is now one of Germany's most popular tourist attractions. Fantasy Castle (right) is the creation of Walt Disney, and delights visitors to Disneyland in southern California.

Modern knights

Knights no longer fight on the battlefield. Instead, enthusiasts dress up in armor and demonstrate knights' skills to entertain crowds. Castles that are open to the public stage displays of jousting on horseback, and archers shooting with bows and arrows. Guests may enjoy a medieval-style banquet in the castle hall.

The **Alhambra** in Granada, Spain, was built by the Moors between 1248 and 1354 and contains many fine examples of Moorish art. The Alhambra was the last stronghold of the Moors against the Christians. In 1492 it was captured by Spanish armies.

CASTLE FACTS

- **The biggest castle is Prague Castle in the Czech Republic. You could fit 13 football fields inside its walls!**

- **The widest moats surround the Imperial Palace in Beijing, China. They are 150 feet (46 meters) wide.**

- **The biggest castle still used as a residence is Windsor Castle in England, used as a home by Queen Elizabeth II.**

French castles are among the most beautiful in the world. This splendid castle-palace near Tours, France, was built across a river in the 1500's, as a luxurious home for a noble family.

Glossary

archbishop A bishop of the highest rank.

bailey Outer wall of a castle or a court inside the walls.

barons High-ranking nobles.

branding Burning a mark on the skin with a hot iron.

breeches Trousers reaching to just below the knee.

broch Ancient stone-built tower.

coronation Ceremony in which a ruler is crowned.

Crusades Series of wars fought in the Middle East by Christians from Europe against Muslims.

fallow Land left untilled or unsown for a time to allow the soil to recover.

feudalism Social and political system of Europe during the Middle Ages. Under this system, a lord provided protection for the peasants who worked for him.

fief Land held in return for military service.

Franks People of Europe living in what is now France and Germany. The Frankish kingdom was the most powerful Christian kingdom of western Europe in the early Middle Ages.

frescoes Pictures painted on damp plaster of walls.

friar A man who belongs to a religious order of the Roman Catholic Church.

gargoyle A fancy, carved waterspout on the roof or eaves of a building, shaped in the form of a very ugly human or animal figure.

garter A band worn around the leg to hold up a sock or stocking.

guild A union of people in the same trade or craft in the Middle Ages.

herald In the Middle Ages, an officer in charge of all the etiquette of chivalry who kept records of the arms of the nobles.

hermit A person who lives alone and away from other people, especially for religious reasons.

illuminated Describes books decorated with colored lettering or illustrations.

keep The strongest part or main tower of a castle.

manor A large estate owned by a lord in the Middle Ages. Peasants lived on part of this land in return for goods, services, or rent.

manuscript A page or pages written by hand.

minstrel A professional entertainer, who played and sang and recited poems.

moat Deep, wide trench filled with water, dug around a castle or town to keep enemies out.

monastery House or group of buildings in which monks live, work, and pray together.

Mongols People of Mongolia, followers of Genghis Khan.

monk A man who belongs to a religious order, and lives in a monastery.

Moors People from North Africa, who conquered and lived in parts of Spain from 711 to 1492.

Muslims People who follow the religion of Islam, founded by Muhammad.

parchment The hide of a sheep, goat, or other animal that has been dried and prepared as a writing surface.

peasant Someone who works on a small farm, or the owner of a small farm.

pharmacist A person trained to prepare medicine and drugs.

pilgrim A person who travels to an important holy place, such as a shrine, for a religious purpose.

Pope The leader of the Roman Catholic Church.

prefabricated Ready-made parts, for assembling later.

Romanesque Style of architecture between that of ancient Roman and Gothic, noted for round arches and vaults.

scribe A person employed to do writing.

shrine A place, such as a tomb or chapel, where holy objects are kept.

stained glass Colored glass used to make decorative windows.

stocks A wooden frame with holes in which the ankles, or ankles and wrists, of a person were locked to punish him or her for a crime.

tapestry Decorated woven cloth used for wall-coverings, furniture, or windows.

tournament Series of military exercises in which knights fought to show off their skill and courage.

troubadour Poet who wrote love songs. Troubadours were popular in Europe from the 1000's to the 1200's.

tumbler An acrobat.

turret A small tower usually on the corner of a building.

vassal A person who held land from a superior and swore loyalty in return.

Vikings Warriors and sailors from Scandinavia who made long voyages and raided the coasts of Europe from the 700's to the 1000's.

Index A page number in **bold** type indicates a picture

Acknowledgments
Cover: Alcazar Castle, Segovia, Spain (Steve Elmore, West Stock)
Back Cover: Gauntlet (Metropolitan Museum of Art, New York City)
4 *September* by the Limbourg brothers, from the Duc de Berry's *Les Très Riches Heures*, Musée Condé, Chantilly, France. 6 Bord Fáilte Eireann; Detail of Bayeux Tapestry (1000's-1100's) from Bayeux Museum, France (Barnaby's Picture Library, London). 7 L.L.T. Rhodes from Nancy Palmer. 8 Edmond Nagele, The Photo Source. 10 Archives Générales du Royaume, Brussels; ZEFA. 11 Adeline Haaga, Tom Stack & Assoc. 12 *March* from the Duc de Berry's *Les Très Riches Heures*, Musée Condé, Paris (Giraudon). 13 Detail of a manuscript (1400's), Bettmann Archive. 14 Illustration from *The Hours of the Virgin* (1500's) by an unknown Flemish artist, Pierpoint Morgan Library, New York City. 16 From *A Boy's King Arthur* by Sidney Lanier, illustrated by N.C. Wyeth © 1917 by Charles Scribner's Sons and used by permission of the publisher. 18 Pierpoint Morgan Library, New York City. 19 The Metropolitan Museum of Art, New York City. 20 Scottish Tourist Board. 21Detail of an illuminated manuscript, Masters and Fellows of Corpus Christi College, Cambridge University, England; drawing (1457) by Hektor Muelch, Archiv für Kunst und Geschichte. 22 Detail from an illuminated manuscript, Bibliothèque Nationale, Paris. 23 Detail from an illuminated manuscript, Bibliothèque Nationale, Paris; illustration by an unknown artist from the *Stumpf Chronicle* , Zentralbibliothek, Zurich, Switzerland. 25 ZEFA. 26 Manuscript illustration (1300's), British Library; Photo Trends. 27 Detail of French manuscript (about 1450), Granger Collection; Michael Freeman, Bruce Coleman Ltd; detail of stained glass window (about 1200) in Strasbourg Cathedral, France (Ronald Sheridan). 28 Bodleian Library, Oxford; English manuscript (about 1450) Granger Collection. 29 From the Harley manuscript of *Froissart's Chronicles*, British Library, London. 30 Mary Evans Picture Library; Dean and Chapter of Lincoln Cathedral. 31 Warwick Castle. 32 Detail of an illumination from *The Vigils of Charles VII* (1400's) Bibliothèque Nationale, Paris. 33 Culver; Fionnbar Callanan. 34 Bruno Barbey, Magnum; fresco (1200's) in the Holy Cave, Subiaco, Italy (SCALA/Art Resource). 35 Illumination by a Persian artist, The Metropolitan Museum of Art, New York City (Werner Forman Archive); detail of manuscript (1400's) Bibliothèque Nationale, Paris. 36 © Ronald Sheridan. 37 Detail from manuscript (1448), National Library of Austria, Vienna; Michael Holford. 38 WORLD BOOK photo by Leonard von Matt; painting by Simon Marmion (about 1450-1500), Henry E. Huntingdon Library, San Marino, California. 39 From the Ellesmere manuscript, Henry E. Huntingdon Library, San Marino, California; Haesler Art Publishers/Art Resource; Michael Holford. 40*The Attainment: The Vision of the Holy Grail* (1896) detail of a tapestry by Sir Edward Burne-Jones, Birmingham Museums and Art Gallery, England; illustration from a French manuscript (about 1300), Bodleian Library, Oxford, England. 41 Detail of oil painting (1917) by N.C.Wyeth (Brandywine River Museum, Chadds Ford, Pa.); detail of woodcut, Granger Collection; Illustration from a manuscript in the British Museum, London (Granger Collection).42 Detail of a painting (1400's) by Jean Mielot (Bettmann Archive); Bibliothèque Nationale, Paris; Trinity College, Dublin, Ireland, The Green Studio Ltd. 43 BBC Hulton; detail of a manuscript (about 1300), International College of Surgeons Museum, Chicago, WORLD BOOK photo. 44 Manuscript illustration from *De Rege Johanne* (early 1300's), British Library. 45 French tapestry and detail (late 1400's), The Metropolitan Museum of Art, New York City, Gift of John D. Rockefeller, Jr.,The Cloisters Collection, 1937; illustration from *A Dissertation on the Pageants...* by Thomas Sharp, courtesy Oscar G. Brockett. 46 Mural (about 1350), Ørslev Church near Sorø, Denmark (National Museum, Copenhagen); detail of relief sculpture by Luca della Robbia (SCALA/Art Resource). 47 Detail from French manuscript (early 1300's), Granger Collection; miniature (early 1300's) by an unknown Swiss painter, Heidelberg University Library. 48 Detail of *Lady in Yellow* (about 1465) by Alesso Baldovinetti, National Gallery, London; *Lady with a Pink* by Hans Memling, The Metropolitan Museum of Art, New York City, the Jules S. Bache Collection, 1949. 49 Detail of *Elderly Couple* by Jan Gossaert, National Gallery, London (Raymond V. Schoder, S.J.); French manuscript (1200's), © Pierpoint Morgan Library, New York City; detail of manuscript *Le Roman de la Rose*, Bibliothèque Nationale, Paris (Hubert Josse); detail of painted chest, Accademia di Firenze, Florence (Hubert Josse). 50 Hanford Photography, from the Church of St. Mary, Stoke D'Abernon, England; Biblioteca Estense, Modena, Italy (SCALA/EPA). 51 Manuscript illustration (1300's) Bibliothèque Nationale, Paris. 53 Bayeux Museum, Bayeux, France (SCALA/Art Resource). 54 Art Resource; *St. Francis in Ecstasy* (about 1480) © The Frick Collection, New York City. 55 Detail of an illuminated manuscript, Bodleian Library, Oxford, England; as p.32. 56 Fionnbar Callanan; Crown copyright. 58 ZEFA. 59 Gerald Cubitt, Bruce Coleman; Robert Harding Picture Library. 60 Vance Henry, Taurus; © David Pollack, The Stock Market.; Phil and Loretta Hermann. Hillstrom Stock Photo. 61 © Adam Woolfitt, Woodfin Camp, Inc.; © Tetrel/ Explorer from Photo Researchers.

Illustrations
By WORLD BOOK artists including Robert Addison, Zorica Dabich, Linden Artists, H. Charles McBarron, Jr., Taka Murakami, Oxford Illustrators, Allan Phillips, George Suyeoka.